101 Boobilicious Moments

by Michelle F. Creeden

Illustrated by Kaitlin Rim

Designed by Rachel Michele Davis

DORRANCE
PUBLISHING CO
EST. 1920
PITTSBURGH, PENNSYLVANIA 15238

Dorrance Publishing Co
585 Alpha Drive
Suite 103
Pittsburgh, PA 15238
Visit our website at www.dorrancebookstore.com

ISBN: 978-1-4809-5850-0
eISBN: 978-1-4809-5873-9

Always consult with your doctor regarding the health and safety of you and your baby. There is no one right way to feed a baby. I am not a doctor, although I have been known to heal several ouchies with a kiss. I am a mom, a mom with a dream of helping other moms. This book is about breastfeeding, but I hope to hit a funny bone for all readers.

Michelle F. Creeden

You know you're a breastfeeding mom when...

Chapter 1
Nursing State of Affairs

After you give birth, you feel contractions while breastfeeding.

Hello, uterus, returning to pre-pregnancy size!

You have your favorite nursing station in the house.

#3

Your baby is either a speed eater or a casual diner.

#4

You nurse with the company of four-legged friends.

#5

You nurse, even when you're feeling under the weather.

#6

You've grabbed anything for privacy while nursing: a restaurant napkin, a pillow, a magazine... just to cover your girls up a bit.

It's like an Olympic sport.

#8

You want your baby to focus
on the task at hand.

Your baby sucks on anything, hoping for milk to come out.

#10

You breastfeed everywhere!

In the back of a car. In a bathroom stall. On the beach!

#11

You breastfeed doing almost anything!

Catching up with friends. Reading a recipe. Getting shoes on!

#12

As soon as you're in a comfortable position,

20 MINUTES LATER

the baby is done nursing.

#13

Running errands is finely calculating around feeding times.

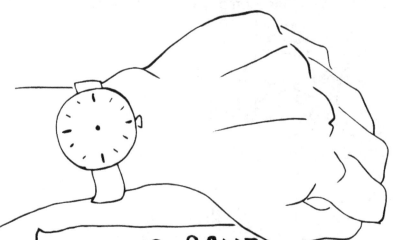

TODAYS SCHEDULE

7:00AM . . . . WAKE UP

8:30AM . . . . . . GROCERIES

10:00AM BREASTFEED!

12:00PM . . . . . NOURISH SELF

1:00PM . . . . BIRTHDAY PARTY

4:00PM BREASTFEED!

5:30PM . . . . . NOURISH FAMILY

7:00PM WORK THOSE BOOBIES!

10:00PM THANK GOD, SLEEP...

Your baby points to what they want.

You use your baby as an excuse
to leave an unwanted conversation.

#16

You have a staring contest with your baby.

They are done nursing but are still latched,
and you're waiting for them to unlatch.

Chapter 2

Sleep or Lack Thereof

#17

You nurse more than you...

sleep.

#18

You can only sleep comfortably...

on your back.

#19

You wake up one minute before your baby does in the middle of the night because your boobs can sense it.

Boob ESP!

#20

You try not
to fall asleep
in the rocking chair.

Chapter 3

Food! Because Mom Gets Hungry, Too

#21

You're hungrier breastfeeding than when you were pregnant.

#22

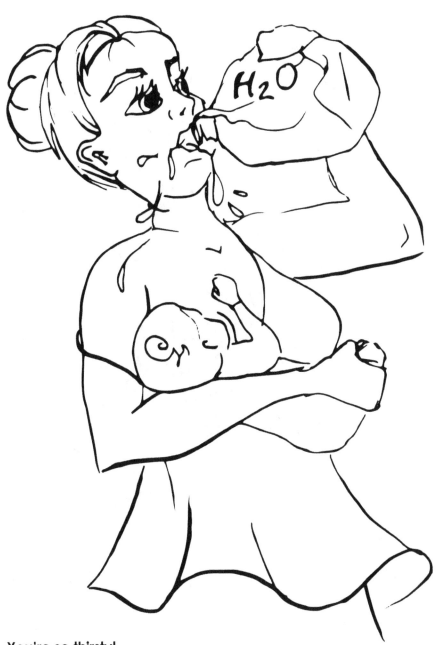

You're so thirsty!

You become good at eating with your non-dominant hand.

Chapter 4
Milk, Precious Milk

You do cry over spilled milk.

Your freezer has no room for food.

#26

One ounce of milk is just as precious as five.

#27

You've Googled home remedies to use your breastmilk.

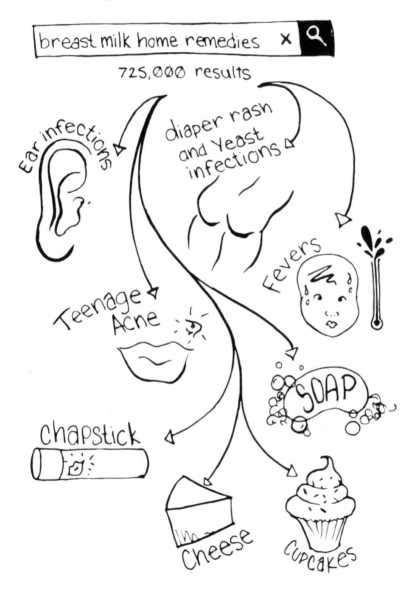

Some you've tried, some you didn't.

#28

You can tell how many ounces are in each boob...

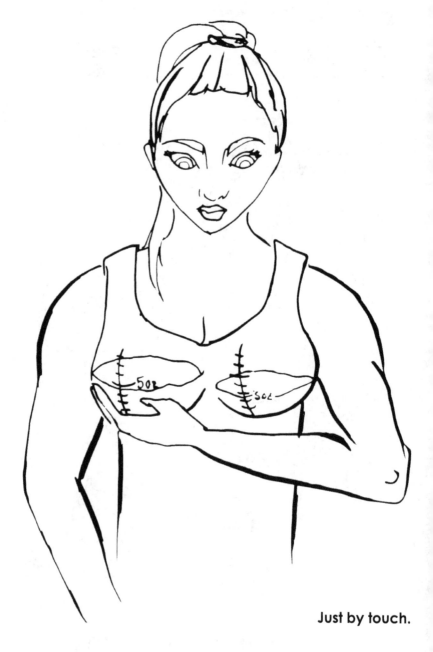

Just by touch.

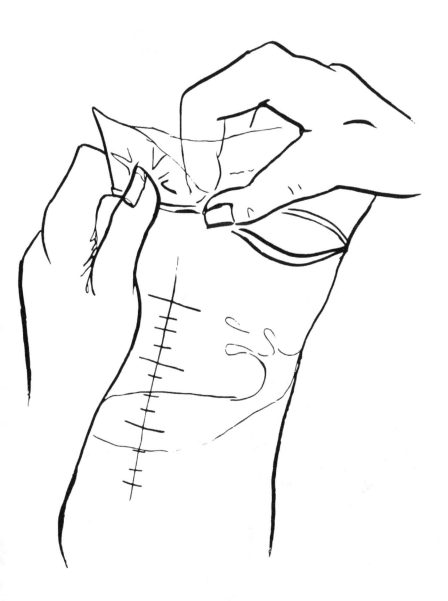

You triple check that
the storage bags are securely sealed.

#30

You'll grab any container to collect the milk that's leaking.

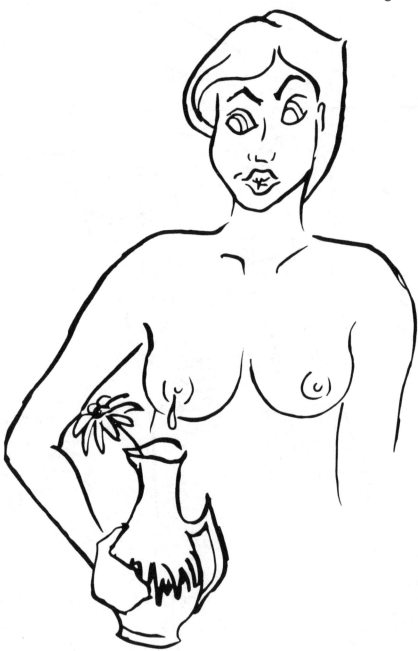

#31

When preparing a pumped bottle
for your baby, you are careful to...

Swirl, not shake.

#32

You have your built-up supply
on a fine-tuned rotation schedule.

#33

You are curious about the fat content of your milk

and check in the fridge to see the separation.

Chapter 5

To the Person
You Say "I Do" To

You've made your husband taste your milk.

#35

You sometimes wish your husband had boobs.

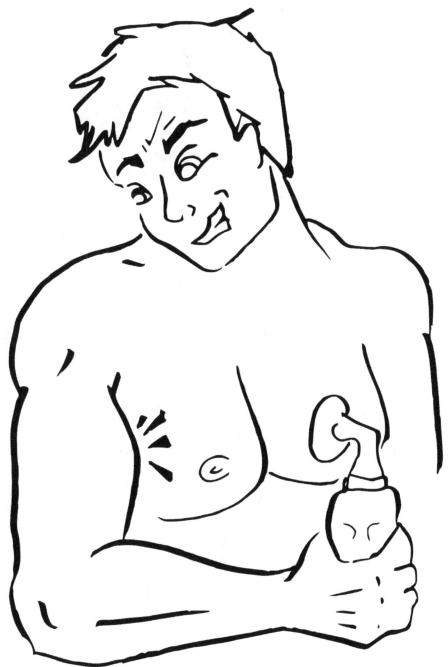

#36

Your baby can lift your shirt up
faster than your hubby.

#37

What used to hold allure

now doesn't.

#38

He's your delivery boy when you forgot something...

and the baby is already latched.

#39

You appreciate his support!

Chapter 6

Working Momma

#40

You debate whether to wake your baby to feed,

or let him sleep and pump at work.

You time pump breaks around meetings.

You have a pump break checklist.

Work is stressful

and you're having

a hard time to let down.

#44

You know that when you walk to where you pump,

all of your coworkers know what you're about to do.

#45

If you pump in your work's parking lot,

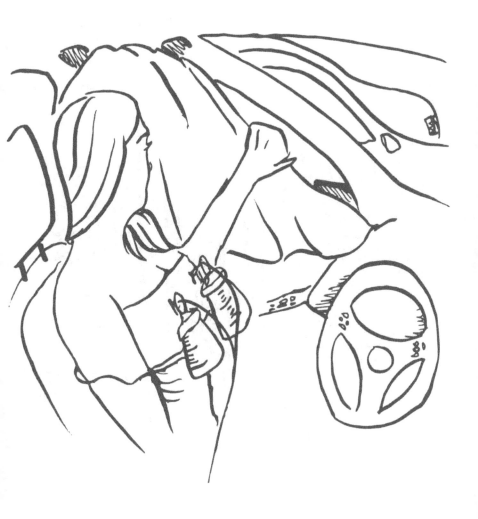

You've made little window curtains for your car for privacy.

#46

If the designated pump area isn't available,

IT sets you up in the electrical server room.

If you work at home

and pump at your desk,

you accommodate

for meetings

and phone calls.

Chapter 7

The P-U-M-P

#48

You stare at the two shields,
trying to figure out which size you are.

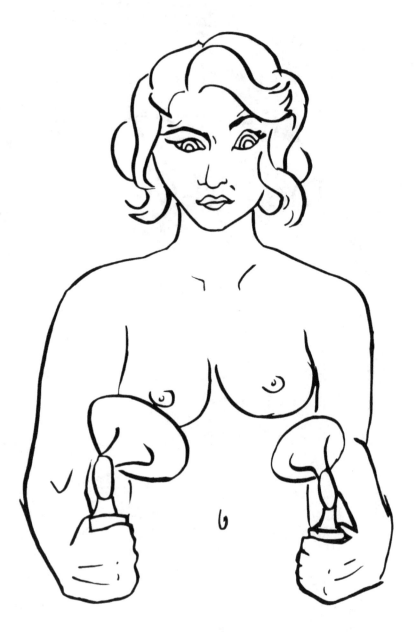

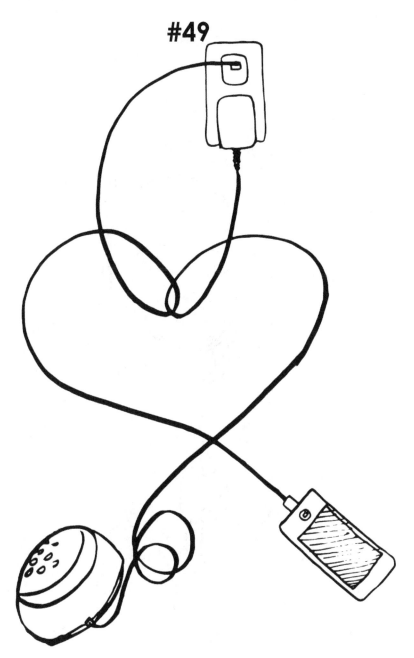

Your phone charger and pump charger
are on the same level of importance.

You come up with a song
to the rhythm of your pump.

#51

You lose count of how many times
you've washed your pump.

#52

You put the pump down and squeeze
because you can milk yourself better.

Your pump bag becomes...

your purse.

BABY

BOTTLES, PACIFIER, BIB
TISSUES, CHANGE
BOOK, WIPES, OF CLOTHES,
DIAPERS, CHANGING
BREAST PUMP!

DIAPER RASH
CREAM,
FAVORITE
TOY

MOMMY
WALLET
WATER
KEYS
CHAPSTICK

You wonder if Madonna came up with
her cone boob look from a hands-free nursing top.

Chapter 8

Wardrobes
and Malfunctions

You're not sure how long you were walking around the house

with one boob hanging out.

#56

You want to look nice, but not too nice
in case you get thrown up on.

#57

Your clothes fit differently throughout the day.

Your shirt is stiff where the milk leaked.

You choose your outfit based
on the accessibility of your boobs.

Chapter 9

Weaning -
A Love/Hate
Relationship

#60

Weaning can be just as difficult.

To pump or not to pump.

#62

WOoHOOO!

You are looking forward

to the freedom

but will miss breastfeeding.

You're not exactly sure what
you'll do with that extra time!

Chapter 10

Boob Pains and Other
Body Oddities

Nipple cream and cooling packs are your best friends.

#65

Nipples are ready to go at all times!

#66

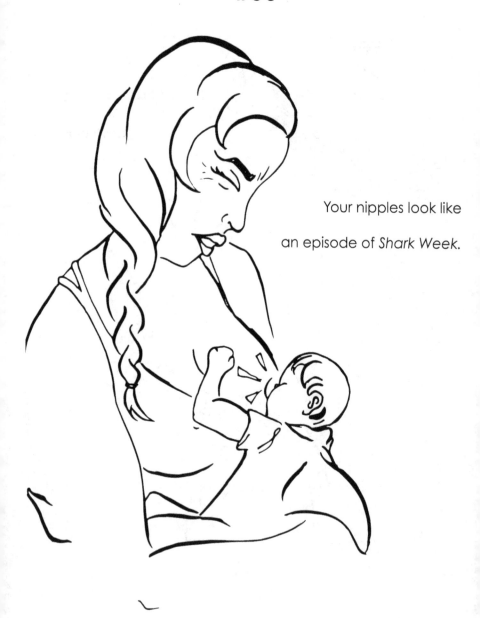

Your nipples look like

an episode of *Shark Week*.

#67

You don't want

to wear a bra.

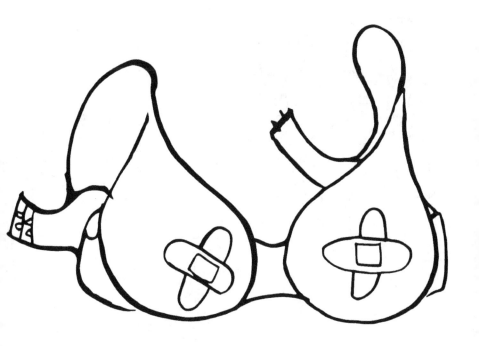

#68

You can bounce a quarter off your boob

if you haven't nursed in several hours.

#69

You ask people not to hug you too tightly.

#70

They bite down ever so slightly just to see your reaction.

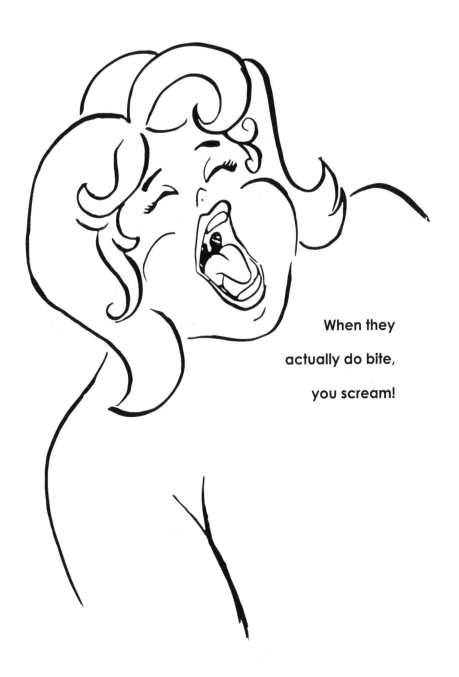

When they
actually do bite,
you scream!

#72

Some days,
well, you just
feel like...

a cow.

You spray.

#75

You leak.

#76

You shower with your back to the water because your nipples are so sensitive.

Your arm loses feeling.

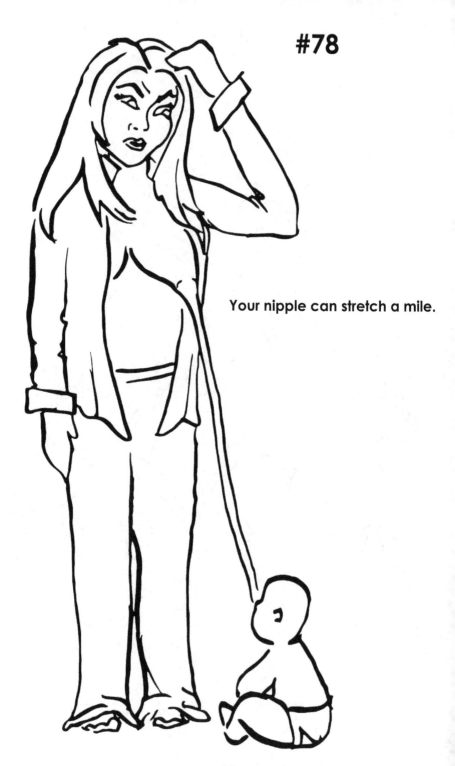

Your nipple can stretch a mile.

#79

Your boobs are
lopsided because
 your baby prefers
one side over
the other.

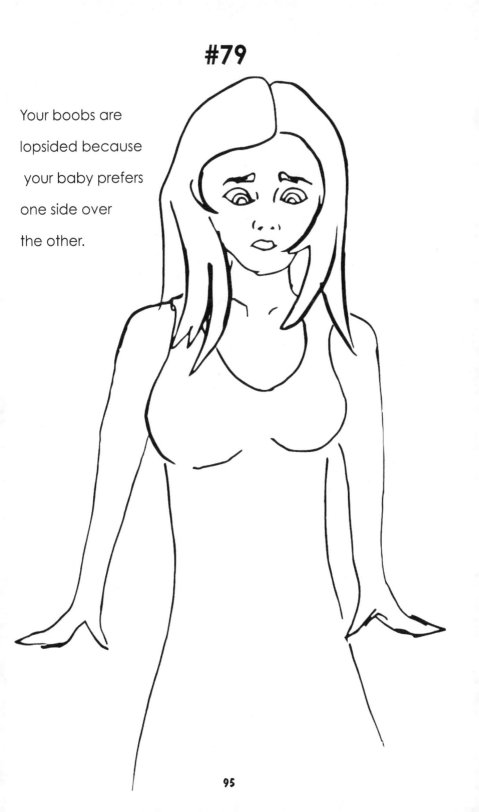

Hearing another baby cry could set you off.

Your armpits itch while your baby nurses.

#82

You check with your doctor
to find out what medications
you can and cannot take.

Chapter 11

Boobilicious Moments

#83

Your kitchen counter looks like an aisle
in a baby department store.

#84

You take a selfie while breastfeeding

because you are curious

what you look like in action.

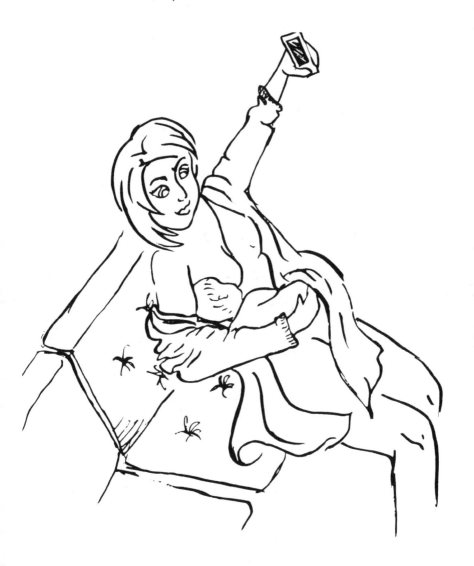

You have a lactation consultant on speed dial.

#86

You've tasted your own milk out of curiosity.

You send pumped-bottle pictures
to your friends to show proud
and not-so-proud bottles.

#88

Your baby looks at other women's boobs.

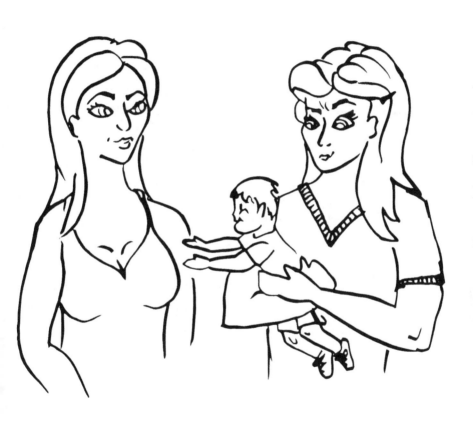

Chapter 12
Self-Love

#89

You are happy

you can provide your child

with all the health benefits breastmilk provides.

You do your best

to eat healthy for you

and your baby.

#91

You care less about what others think.

You hope you inspire

other mothers to breastfeed.

#93

You feel empowered.

Chapter 13

Baby Love

#94

Your baby plays with your hair while nursing.

#95

You wonder what they dream about

after they unlatch, with a huge smile on their face.

#96

You can solve all of your baby's

troubles with **one latch.**

#97

Those baby covers

become a game of peek-a-boo

and peek-a-boob.

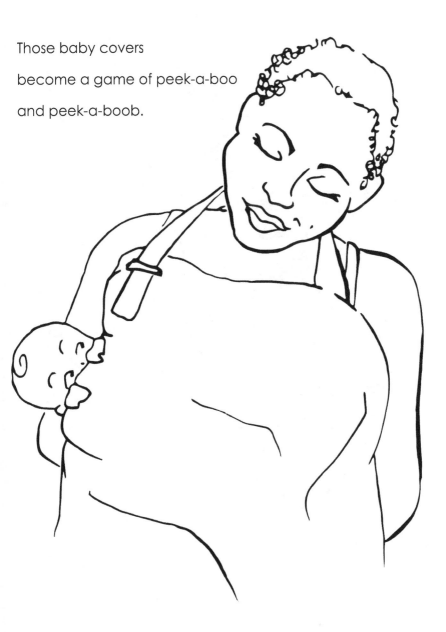

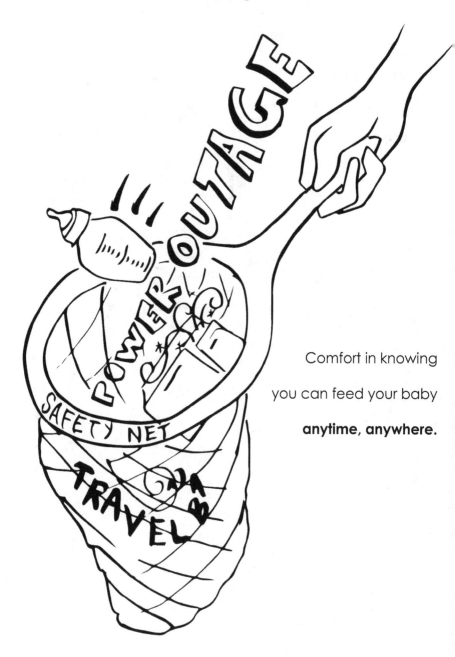

Comfort in knowing

you can feed your baby

anytime, anywhere.

#99

You catch yourself staring

at your child, and your heart

is overflowing **with love!**

#100

They hug you.

Full-on body hug.

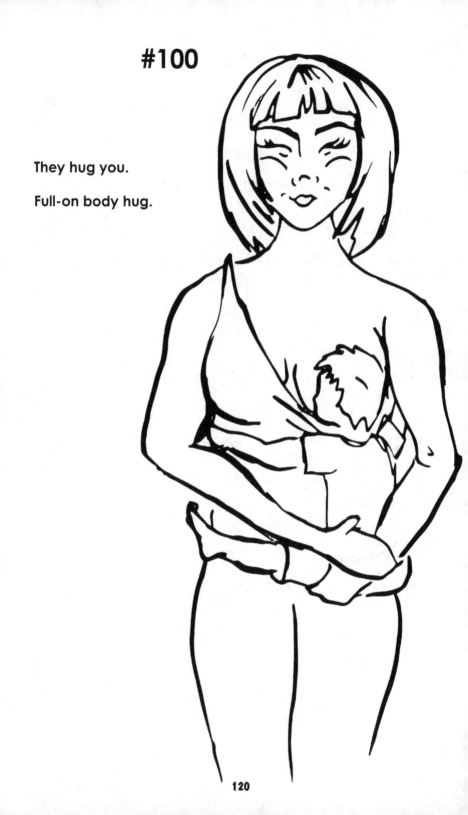

#101

You'll cherish the memories

for a lifetime of these

boobilicious moments.

CPSIA information can be obtained
at www.ICGtesting.com
Printed in the USA
LVHW03s1618200918
590799LV00009B/460/P